BEWARE THE CATFISHER

MY JOURNEY WITH ONLINE DATING

BRENDA LEE ACHESON

Beware the Catfisher
Copyright © 2020 by Brenda Lee Acheson

All rights reserved. No part of this publication may be reproduced, distributed, or transmitted in any form or by any means, including photocopying, recording, or other electronic or mechanical methods, without the prior written permission of the author, except in the case of brief quotations embodied in critical reviews and certain other non-commercial uses permitted by copyright law.

Tellwell Talent
www.tellwell.ca

ISBN
978-0-2288-2589-0 (Hardcover)
978-0-2288-2588-3 (Paperback)
978-0-2288-2590-6 (eBook)

Table of Contents

Introduction v

Chapter 1: My Online Dating Profile and Chosen Dating Sites 1
Chapter 2: Initial Contacts That Were Clearly Fishing 3
Chapter 3: First Contact 5
Chapter 4: Second Contact 11
Chapter 5: Third Contact 31
Chapter 6: More Men 35
Chapter 7: Warning Signs 43
Chapter 8: What to Do If You Suspect You Are Being Groomed 47
Chapter 9: Stop and Think about What Is Being Said to You 49
Chapter 10: Call the Catfisher Out 51
Chapter 11: How to Extract Yourself from Catfishing 53
Chapter 12: Forgive Yourself 55
Chapter 13: How to Protect Yourself 57
Chapter 14: Closure 59

Disclaimer 61

Introduction

I do not think I am outside of the normal range of people who look for someone on the online dating sites. I'm in my 50s and single; I have never been married and have no children and I'm employed. I'm honest about the fact I'm overweight but I'm active.

I started looking online again after ending a nine-year relationship with a man I met and fell in love with on the online dating site Match.com. I took a year off from the end of that relationship so I did not jump into another one and put myself at risk of doing something stupid or being too vulnerable. When I originally started online dating, I did have to negotiate through a lot of people who were not what they claimed to be and now I know they were what is called a Catfisher.

Catfishing is an interesting word, but what does it mean? Catfishing is when someone creates a fake online identity, hoping to lure people into some sort of online relationship, often romantic, with the ultimate goal being to steal their money or identity for fraudulent purposes. They usually use social media networks, dating sites and any types of online forums that may work for them.[1]

---

[1] www.elitepersonalfinance.com/catfishing-scam/

A Catfisher can be either male or female or even be someone pretending to be the opposite sex.

I am not a rich person. I am not what I consider gorgeous (as one called me). I consider myself average, overweight, intelligent and not as vulnerable to fraud as someone might think. I tend to be a thinker and ask questions, but still I have been Catfished. I did not fall for the bait that was used and did not send money. But still I had hoped the Catfishers were real and was disappointed when I found out they were not.

As an important part of my story, I am including excerpts from my personal journal so you can see what goes on in someone's mind when these Catfishers get into it. The emotions and hope are real but the relationship is not.

Initially, I did not plan to write a book about my experiences with online dating, but I was keeping a journal (something I had done in the past) just for my own records. I found myself dealing with people who were clearly Catfishers a number of times, which made me think there must be books and articles about it. Sadly, I realized there was not a lot of information on Catfishing.

I continued contact with some of the people I thought might be Catfishers until I felt certain that they were. There is still one person I am in contact with, and I am still unsure if he is a Catfisher or not. My intentions were not to use these people for my own profit (this book); my goal was truly to find someone for a relationship.

I have written this book to help people avoid being a victim of these low lives with no conscious. If I help even one person, I am happy to do so.

Chapter 1

My Online Dating Profile and Chosen Dating Sites

Ten years ago, I met my former partner on Match.com, so my first thought was to use that site again. Since then, Match.ca was up and running so I hoped that that would limit the number of non-Canadian people and contact with scammers. Unfortunately, that was not the case.

When I wrote my online dating profile, I was honest. I do not believe in creating a false profile because eventually you have to tell the truth. Why start with lies? I had just turned 58. I have never been married but had ended a nine-year relationship. I had no children. I listed my occupation, a writer. I added a couple of recent photographs, again no point in pretending I still look like I did in my 20s or 30s. I was very specific about what and who I was looking for as well as what I did not want. I did this with all the sites I eventually registered with.

After a couple of weeks of non-activity or interest on my part, I expanded to some other sites such as eHarmony, Silver Singles, Senior Chat City, Elite Singles, Date Over 60, Over 55 Singles and Dating for Seniors. This may sound like a lot of work, but each site seemed to bring me waves of interest and then quiet.

I did correspond with multiple people at the same time. Most of them were not where I lived, so it was highly unlikely anything was going to come from these conversations. If it became clear over time that the person was a Catfisher or untruthful, I ended contact with them.

Based on my experiences, I do not think any one site is better than another. I think they all have their scammers and liars, and you have to take what people say about themselves with some skepticism. Some sites seemed to be better than others at matching me with people I would be interested in while other sites seem to totally miss the mark!

I truly wanted my profile to stand out by being honest about who I was and what I was looking for. Catfishers are looking for a specific type of profile and mine seemed to fit it repeatedly.

What do I think they saw in my profile that caught their interest? I think it was my age (58), that I had never been married and that I did not have children. I am assuming they thought I was lonely and vulnerable (which I was not). They knew I was employed and had listed hobbies such as travelling, which may have given the appearance of having money. All those who contacted me wanted to know more about where I had been travelling and how long it was since my last trip.

Catfishers can be male or female, but I was never aware of being contacted by anyone who was female (or at least never got the vibe that they were). I always wondered, especially with the first one that I fell for, if some of the more successful Catfishers are female because they would know what would interest and get another woman's attention and affection. Most people I have talked to think Catfishers are primarily male and their female counterparts are Golddiggers. The consensus among my friends is that the Golddiggers were more easily recognized by others but not the person involved with them. I think the same could be said for Catfishers as emotions blind you from what may be obvious to others.

Chapter 2

Initial Contacts That Were Clearly Fishing

Within the first 10 minutes of my Match.ca profile going live, not one but two people contacted me and they both were clearly fishing. How did I know? In their initial emails, they wanted my personal email address and/or my cellphone number so they could contact me off the dating site. I do not recommend giving out such personal contact information right away, and the dating sites do offer protection from the wrong people getting your personal information. These first two people also gave me way too much information for an initial contact—their entire life story, which included tragedies to evoke an emotional response and connection.

The first two Catfishers also had a common theme that I had seen before. Both were widowers and were self-employed; both did not live anywhere near me so meeting them would be unlikely. I blew them both off, saying that I had read their profiles and was not interested in anyone outside of my area.

The other sites had the same issue: people claiming they were either self-employed or retired, and wanting my personal email and/or phone number to contact off site. My basic response was I do not give out my personal contact information until I meet someone in person. The clear Catfishers would then stop contact immediately.

Some of the dating sites actually were good about telling me that someone was suspicious and to not continue any contact with them. I appreciated the sites doing that but always wondered what the people had done that caused the site to identify them.

Excerpts from My Journal: August 2, 2019

Although I was in contact with other people, I joined other dating sites in order to keep my options open. So far, I have had another 4 questionable contacts that I'm sure were catfish attempts.

Today one contacted me and his profile said he was in Fort McMurray. After I rejected him, he wanted me to give my email to him and I said no I don't give it out until I physically meet someone. Then his profile location changed to Toronto. Strange behaviour so I am glad I rejected him. There have been way too many asking for texting or emailing private information and sorry I'm not going that route again unless I meet the person.

Chapter 3

First Contact

Chris and I met on Match.ca and had an instant connection. He did not say that he was a widower or that he was self-employed, and he gave me no reason to think he was not real. The photograph of him on the site was not someone I would initially be attracted to, but I thought, "Why not?"

Chris/Francis the first photograph I received in which he looks the age he said he was.

After a few emails exchanges within the site, he asked for my personal contact information because it would be easier to chat. I was interested so I thought, "Why not?" He lived two hours away from me, so I gave him my cell number and my email address.

Once we started chatting off the site, he gave me his full name, which was not Chris, and he never explained the different name of Francis instead of Chris. We also exchanged email addresses, and when he sent me his first email, it had his company name on the signature line. I looked up the company name and it had what looked like a legitimate site. I also looked him up on LinkedIn, FaceBook and other media sites. All seemed legitimate.

What attracted me to Chris/Francis was that he was articulate, and he said he did not realize he wanted someone until we started chatting and were very open with each other. He then told me that he was a widower and had lost his wife and only child, a daughter, a few years earlier in a car accident.

We were texting and emailing throughout the day, getting to know each other and our routines. We tried talking on the phone one night, but it was stormy and did not work well. But oh my god, what a sexy deep voice with an accent! I called him "my sweet man" and he called me "his baby."

We exchanged photographs and he is very masculine and has a gorgeous smile. But the first hint that he wasn't who he claimed he was is that the photo on the site looked nothing like the photos he sent me. Of course, with this sort of situation I have some doubts until we physically meet, which he promised next week, so I did not talk about him to anyone. If all this is true, the irony is that he is in the jewelry business and I don't wear any jewelry. He did not come out and said he has money, but he did ask me a question that I think was an attempt to see where money fits into my views of importance.

Excerpts from My Journal: August 10, 2019

He left for a business trip today and texted me to let me know he was thinking of me and was between flights. I was on a road trip in the back seat of my sister's SUV so I told him he could ask me questions while he waited for his next flight. So, he did until he boarded his next flight and told me he would text on the next leg. He asked me if I saw myself living in a warmer climate in the future. I said I would love that when I retired. He owns property in the Bahamas. So even though I have doubts, I really hope this is real. I look at his pictures and I just cannot stand it—he's so good looking and his smile just is so nice. I told him I love his smile because it exudes so much positive energy and warmth. I will be so disappointed if it's not real!

I've also been chatting with two other men, one in Calgary and one in Texas. They are both very nice but we have not gotten to the same sort of connection as the first one.

One Sunday was an interesting one. The one I've been texting and emailing seems to be legit and from our emails and conversations we had connected majorly! He and I have both said we are open to each other and have said we love each other. I was still guarding myself from it not being legit but felt if it was, I would have considered something permanent with him. I probably knew more about him in the last two weeks than I did with my ex in six months. He was supposed to be back from his trip on Thursday and we are supposed to meet on the weekend but that didn't happen.

I found it very strange to have such a strong attraction to someone based only on the words he was saying to me.

Excerpts from My Journal: August 17, 2019

He said something today that I thought wow he's serious or he's very good. I said I needed to get propane for my BBQ and he said, "I should be there to do that for you." I thought okay let's see if he's serious. I went out and did some running around and when he texted me to see how I was doing I told him I had gone out but had not gotten propane so he could do that. He said, "Good the propane is on me when I'm back." He also hinted he wants me to relax. I think he thinks I do too much outside of work. I know he says he cooks but not sure about anything else.

I asked for an updated photo of his smile. So far, I ask for something, I get it. I keep looking at his picture and hoping he's real! Physically I am so attracted to him and from everything he has told me about himself we would be totally compatible. Fingers crossed we meet and I find out if it was BS or the truth.

In case it is BS with him I'm still chatting with the other 2 guys. The one in Calgary is friendly and we've started asking questions back and forth. He's hinted he'd like to get together and I've said yes but haven't pushed it. I really want to meet the other guy first!

The one from Texas seems to be really interested and I did give him my cell number, even calling, but I think he's bogus. He sounds like he's a black guy. I gave him the excuse I have a headache and going back to bed. He just texted. He's mothering me. Second man today doing that!

Me and the first guy have closed out Match profiles and I had registered with another site which I've had nothing happen on. The second guy's profile is still up and he's looking still.

The third guy, from Texas, his name is Tim, I met through Pinterest so very random.

Excerpts from My Journal: August 23, 2019

Well the saying is if it's too good to be true has been going through my head with regards to the first guy, Chris/Francis. Yes, I fell for the BS but wasn't 100 per cent invested because there were a lot of inconsistencies I couldn't ignore. Timeframes that didn't match, pet names that weren't consistent, repeatedly asking the same questions within a short timeframe. It just started falling apart and I lost feelings I had before he even asked for money. Today he *asked and I said I wasn't comfortable with doing it. Pulled on the heartstrings and I thought I'd test it and knew the bank would hold the payment until they talked to me. Totally bogus so I asked that they cancel the payment (how did I know? The name I sent the money to wasn't the name on the account trying to receive it). As soon as it got cancelled a barrage of text messages, I finally said I'm busy and I'll talk to you later. At 4:30 he tried to call and I didn't answer. I'm going to wait until later to tell him "sorry you and the other Chris/Francis aren't getting the money" and then blocking him on my phone and email.*

This is when I started really thinking about writing this book because I never fully believed anything this character said. He was too good to be true and fell for me too quickly. At one point I told him I had never felt this way before and he didn't realize how pissed I was. Now I'm going to have to watch that these people don't use my info and pictures to snare people.

This first experience made me more wary with the other men I was talking to.

Chapter 4

Second Contact

The second person who had contacted me was Will from Calgary. He said he was a widower and that he had his own company. He was not the type of person I am normally attracted to (he had a beard) but he had the best opening line I had ever had or since gotten: "If you were a new menu item at McDonald's, you'd be called McGeorgeous." How could I not respond to something like that?

Excerpts from My Journal August 19, 2019

Meanwhile #2 from Calgary seems to be real but again going in with caution. He seems to be interested but I think he is chatting with multiple people. He contacts me first thing in the morning and at night but it's painfully slow to text with him. He is usually ready to go to bed at 10:00 to 10:30.

Finally, he's doing some pursuing and wanting to meet. Last night he asked what I was doing tonight (Saturday) so I said maybe dinner or a movie. He said, "I was hoping you'd say host me." So, I asked if he'd like me to do that? His response was "YES, YES, YES, YES." I said I liked his enthusiasm so who knows.

Will (that's his name) sends me every morning a beautiful morning greeting. Usually a good night but he's usually distracted. I was ready to write him off when he stepped up and sent some recent photos and told me we'd meet, but he didn't want it to be just coffee he wanted it to be special. So, he's a question.

Will supposedly on his way to his business trip in Turkey.

I am still in contact with Will who is out of the country for 2 plus weeks (his words). If he doesn't ask for "help" financially, I'll be happy but I'm still on the fence with him. Not sure if he's real or not but he's consistent, respectful and has promised we will meet when he gets back. I would love if he's real and we can hook up because he is sweet with his morning greetings and seems "normal."

Excerpts from My Journal: September 9, 2019

Oh my God last night Will finally stepped things up. He texted later than normal and we had a normal conversation and he asked if he could have some mail (a cheque) sent to me to hold until he came back. I said yes *because I know sometimes this is a scam these guys will pull so we will see. We are at week 6 (42 days) since we started chatting so he's moving slow compared to the other ones. Then last night he finally got sexual!*

He said something about "I need more sex" and I said "are you offering" and he said "yes." We then finally made it clear we both want each other. He said I was driving him crazy then we go more explicit. Oh my God it's like he's read my thoughts on what I wanted him to do to me! I don't know if he's real. Oh my God he says he's that good and I'm thinking from what he said I'm in big trouble!

He's hinted in the past about wanting to do more than just coffee when we meet and that he's unique. I'm still not 100 per cent sure if he's real or not. He'll be gone for 2 weeks on Sunday so who knows when he'll be back if he's actually real. I'm just confused after last night ... I was so turned on by him. If he's real I want him to come for the weekend and we either get each other out of each other's system or commit to something. I've re-read our previous conversations and there are so many hints we both want each other but haven't pushed things.

What I love about him is he's consistent. Always in the morning a greeting that brings a smile to my face. At night we ask each other about the other's day. We have never said we love each other but use various emoji to express emotions. So, nothing like the other guys who were scammers, who rushed to say they were in love. Will just says I drive him crazy and it's totally a sexual crazy that I hadn't allowed myself to feel until recently. Just in the last week I've been fantasizing about him very vivid which is very different for me.

I would totally consider being with Will especially if he's as good in bed as he says and sounds like. I know from what he's told me he is a worker too and normal!

I guess time will tell. I'm just hoping he's not another one that's too good to be true and isn't.

These guys being Catfishers has been a fear with all the guys I was in contact with. And the more we chatted back and forth, the harder it becomes to try to keep myself from using some common sense with things that are said.

Excerpts from My Journal: September 11, 2019

Again, Will stepped things up. He called using Skype so I could see him live but the sound didn't work. He could hear and see me but I could see him but not hear. Wow he's sexy, he's better looking than his pictures. He then texted with another app to chat. He said he was asking about my day and wanted to tell me how he felt about me. He said he thinks I'm kind and have a good heart. That I'm a sweetheart and it's easy to fall for me. Longing to meet and spend quality time together. I told him I think he has a sweet heart and I was beyond ready to meet him. Get to know him and spend time together. He liked that and said "Lovely" and "big hearts Lovely." I added "you are so sexy too!" I admitted a few minutes later that I was falling for him too! He didn't respond so I left it at that and went to sleep.

This morning my good morning message: he has this thing about my eyes and called me beautiful.

I really hope he's real but steeling myself if it's not to be. Time will tell. All I know is if he's a scammer he's invested a lot of time and effort on the chance of getting something.

When we were on Skype, he saw me lie back on my bed which he liked. I said it's a comfy bed so he said "yeah it looked like it—enough space for me?" I said "of course whenever you like!" He responded "oh my my ... that's amazing." Then the comment "you drive me crazy." I said "you are driving me crazy."

It's the truth, I go back and forth on if he's real or not. If what he says is the truth, if he's even who he says he is and what he does. So far, it's been 10 days since he left and he hasn't screwed up the timeframe of where he is supposed to be. The first dumb ass screwed that up within a couple of days plus didn't come back when he said he was. Faked a plane ticket to try and convince me (didn't do it very well).

I just don't know. I know the third one, Tim, I really didn't feel anything for him until towards the end and he pushed too quick for money. I had given him my email address and cell number so we could talk outside of Pinterest on Hangouts. Plus, I never believed who he said he was and when we talked on the phone to me it was a black man's voice.

I'm hoping to hear Will's voice soon and that should clear up some of my doubts. The little bit I did hear sounds like he has an accent—English—and some of his sayings make me think that he could be.

Excerpts from My Journal: September 12, 2019

Well an interesting start to the day, Will with his morning greeting said he was the sky and I was the sun that blinded him with my sweetness and kindness. Then called me beautiful. I just wish I could believe he's real but just can't.

Haven't heard from him yet but can as he's online (10:30 pm our time). So, waiting to hear from him.

Excerpts from My Journal: September 13, 2019

Will Skyped and I got to see and hear him. Oh my God such a hottie! He was showing me his hotel but I was focused on him and said he looked nice and he said "I wanted to look good for you!" Frustrating though the connection was horrible.

Excerpts from My Journal: September 14, 2019

Will finally slipped up. Texted to ask what I was doing today and said he was going to bed. Well I don't think so, not at 5 pm where he's supposed to be.

Any feelings for him —GONE! Now I want revenge. I'm going to play him even more than the first dumb ass!

I was so disappointed in this man that I just stopped responding to him like I normally would. He still sent me the morning messages (which I called my morning smiles).

Excerpts from My Journal: September 21, 2019

Well either Will is truly who and what he says he is or he's sucked me back in. I sort of ignored him for a bit, didn't respond right away, and he came back with saying he hated that we weren't able to talk. He can't stop thinking of me. The message this morning just really has me wondering. He sent this morning's message earlier than he normally does and it was very personal. "I wish you were close so I can see you at will. I wish you were just a walk away or better still, by my side always. Since wishes are not horses, here's wishing you good morning from the other side" ... and a smiley emoji.

I responded 2 minutes later which triggered a chat that we've not had for a while. He said I am always on his mind (keeps repeating this). I admitted he's stolen my mind and heart. I had said I was looking forward to hearing about his trip and he said I would after he gave me a tight hug, "kiss your lips passionately." He said he liked I admitted how I felt and he was glad I said that. That he knew my heart is fragile and he promised to take care of it. I said I wanted the kiss and hug and he would do that and more. I said the more ... "you did make a comment about being the best" so I was looking forward to testing that. Again, he said, "I really am and I'll prove it to you. I have what you'll definitely love. I'll pass the test." So, we chatted for a couple of hours altogether.

Either he's really good or real I still can't decide. In all honesty I hope he's real, he seems to be the right balance for what I want and need. I have a lot of questions if we do meet. He seems to be well educated just from what he *writes and how he writes. Very romantic but also the sexy confidence. Why did he trust me with his cheque? Just so many questions.*

All I know is I have feelings for him, different from the other two-bozos who weren't real. Chris/Francis, it was totally a physical attraction—his smile and his build. Tim, his caring and that he was so into me or so I thought.

Will brings a smile to my face almost every morning. He's a positive when I'm feeling negative. He's a quiet sweet man who I'm sure is a gentleman in everything but the bedroom. He's a reader and from the sounds of it he's like me, reads before bed or watches TV. He says he's drawn to me because I'm a good person open and honest and he has this thing with my eyes. I find him sexy knowing that to look at him he's not my normal type. He has this almost stern look but something in his eyes drew me in. The sexiness also comes from his words. He uses words that wouldn't really get to me. My heart races when I see a message from him. The few times we've Skyped he's so sexy looking and sounding!

I think if we meet, I'm done for. I won't say I've fallen in love with him, but pretty close. Until I know it's real or not, he's not going to get 100 per cent of my heart but I can't stop thinking about him. Plus, I want him bad with his claims, I really want to find out for myself. What happened when we sexted, he told me what he planned to do to me and it's like he read my mind of what I wanted him to do. I can actually think about him and imagine and feel what he says he's going to do. If he's real I'm not going to be happy just hopping into bed with him. He intrigues and excites me!

Before 10 pm he sent a message and I responded but he didn't get back until 1:09 am. So that started a chat. He stated at one point "I am coming to take some time away ... having fun with you"[2]. He asked if he had woken me up and I said no I was awake in bed. Finally, after me telling him I had the cheque on Monday, he asked me to confirm the amount so I asked why he trusted me

---

[2] I'm really not sure if he meant to say this or it was a slip.

with it. So, he said "why wouldn't I?" Then explained "I think you're a really good person. Have a good heart." And he said many more things, and said "I'm impressed. I didn't even hesitate to make you hold it." I said "thank you, I try to be that." He then said "yes it seems like you don't even try. It's in you. I'm really happy to know you ... I care more about what's inside." Finally, at 2:40 he asked if I was tired so said yes. I said I was glad we were able to chat. He said he was glad too. He said, "I want you to have a good night rest and sweet dreams." Then added "I cherish you Brenda."

7:11 am a sweet morning greeting. "Would it be okay if I miss you more today than I did yesterday? Good morning sweetie." My response: "Good morning Will, I wish you didn't have to miss me." Him: "Awwww you're so right. Thanks for being a darling." I replied: "It's easy with you Will." His reply: "mmmm I like that" and sent a kiss which I returned.

I just don't know, it's seeming way too easy and real and I'm falling harder for him. I just know if it's not real it's going to really suck and put me in a dark place. I've opened myself up to way too many people and been disappointed, I hope he doesn't join the list.

He just seems to be a normal decent guy who has these extra little traits that I didn't request or expect. At one point I thought he has taken on a role—my online husband. He texts every morning and every night. I didn't ask him to do that, he just started and I'm not sure how long into things that started. I was looking at past messages and when I asked about getting messages when he was away, he said that wouldn't change while he was away—that he didn't think he'd survive without the contact. I'm thinking I'm his lifeline right now while he's away. I guess I'm going to have to ask him if he's been away working and been distracted by our contact and if maybe we made it worse by not meeting first. Or after we meet is it going to be worse for him if he has to go away again?

He keeps saying I'm always on his mind since he's been there. Even before he left, he was saying that so I think his husband behaviours (he's a widower) have kicked in with me. When we first started texting, I was sure he was texting me and other women at the same time. By the time he did his conference I felt like he didn't have that distraction. So, if he's real (again not 100 per cent sure at this point) he seems to have focused totally on me and his work. I asked if he had gone exploring and he said no, he would when the work was done before he came home. That he would take pictures and tell me about it. So again, am I distracting him or giving him the incentive to focus on the work so he finishes and comes home?

Then the whole idea that he trusted me to have the cheque sent to me. It's a cheque for $185,000. He had it sent to someone he only knows from online texts. How did he make the decision to do that and how did he explain our relationship? He only gave them my first name. So, it makes me wonder: he says he has a security company. Did he have a security check done on me Is that why he trusted me or is it truly based on the personality traits from our conversations?

I keep having doubts so went back into our various conversations to try and figure out if I've missed things that would finally give me the answer: is he real or not? Still can't decide.

Going through texts the day he left, Sunday September 1, 2019, he said he missed me through the night. We hadn't text because of his early flight, he went to bed early.

By the Thursday he said he was dreaming of me.

On the Saturday I asked if he was sleeping okay? He said not the best so far. But it's alright. I said I wished I could help him sleep. His response was: "Wish you could help me too ... nothing I want more."

On Sunday September 8th is when he asked if I would accept and hold some important mail for him. I questioned. He said I want the mail to come to you ... then you'll keep it for me till I get back. Cheque. I said okay. I gave him my address. Then we were talking about my dislike of the cold and he suggested more sex. I asked: "Are you offering the more sex-sexy?" He said "obviously I am LOL." He said he'd love to when he gets back. I said something very much on my mind. His response: "Mmmm sweet. Well get ready ... for the best you've ever had." Which started our first sexting session. He admitted I drive him crazy. That he's craving me. I admitted I was craving him. He finally asked what I was wearing to bed. I told him but if he was there, I'd have nothing on. He said he wanted "to feel you so close. Your naked body on me ... skin to skin. Hold you so tight!"

After that, we moved our conversation to a different app and he tried to Skype a couple of times. The reception was horrible but oh my God! He's so good looking and a nice chest and his voice—nice accent! I'm thinking his move was for privacy reason—for whatever reason the sexting made him decide to go to the other app which I'm fine with.

We have now been in two different time zones for 3 weeks and the last 24 hours is the most we've been able to text. He's supposed to be back this week so fingers crossed we are face to face next weekend!

Excerpts from My Journal: September 23, 2019

The first morning Will missed sending me my morning smile but I know he was online earlier and sent me a message. Hopefully tonight he'll have some news.

I'm just anxious to see what's up. He changed his profile photo on the app we use so I'm hoping that means he actually went out and looked around.

Excerpts from My Journal: September 24, 2019

Sweet and short chat this morning. He confirmed he's almost done with his project ... his words just days! He's such a nice sweet man that I'm hoping he is real.

If he's real I keep wondering why I got so lucky? He totally seems down to earth and I told him that adds to his sexiness. His response was that's so sweet. He liked that I noticed and liked his new photo on the app we use.

I will just be glad when he's back. I'm not sleeping like I should because I want to read his texts. Plus, he's admitted he likes how I make him feel.

Excerpts from My Journal: September 25, 2019

Morning greeting: "Here's wishing one of the kindest and amazing hearts I know, a day that is beautiful in every sense of the word. Good morning."

I just love the few minutes each morning he takes to send a special greeting. At one point I thought he had programmed things to send every day at the same time and always had this symbol on it ♉. But since he's been away it's not the exact time and it's very personal and reflects things he's said in chats to me.

I'm just ready for his trip to end and he has to come and see me. I have a $185,000 reason for him to collect.

Speak of him and who texts? I was just about to go in the shower and he decided to include me in his morning. He's working too (multi-tasking) so not steady but nice to hear from him again today. He's so sweet asking questions to find out about the day. Like I said before it's like he goes into husband mode. I think with me he's comfortable and I'm not demanding so he falls into it. Just a sweetheart. I really hope he's real.

We chatted and then when I told him I was in bed I got his full attention. Lead to sexting for an hour and then a phone call. I think he finally got that he's not going to be dominant in the bedroom. Suffice to say he knows I'm interested and want him.

Excerpts from My Journal: September 26, 2019

This morning greeting: "Here's letting you know that of all the things and humans I care a lot about, you matter a lot and top the list. You're always on my mind. Good morning Sweetie."

He's so sweet and man after last night I know he's going to be something else in bed. Plus, now I know his weaknesses! I go anywhere near certain body parts and he's going to be begging. He's also very suggestable which is interesting. I suggested he'd see stars and he was seeing them.

He was begging for relief on the phone so took him through a couple of scenarios and finally he got relief. So, he knows I'm not inhibited so hopefully that entices him.

Excerpts from My Journal: September 27, 2019

Last night he missed sending a message and was late this morning so I thought he always gives me a morning smile, I'll send him one. This is what I sent: "Hi Will. Just wanted to let you know I'm thinking about you. You are such as special man and I feel lucky to have found you." Half an hour later his response: "Thinking of u keeps me awake. Dreaming of u keeps me asleep. Seeing u soon and being with u will definitely keep me alive." Then: "Thank you for your beautiful message, you fill my heart with so much joy." Then an explanation for not talking to me last night.

Excerpts from My Journal: September 28, 2019

Didn't hear from him during the night but a message a 3:49 am that he was still trying to work out the issue. "Hope you are sleeping tight. Kisses." The message woke me up so I responded: "Hope it gets straightened out soon! Kisses to you." So, then he said: "Oh you're up. Mmmm. How come?" So, I said: "I went to bed early and woke up a bit ago. Thinking and dreaming about you." His response: "Awwww always so sweet ... I can't get enough of you. I adore you Brenda." I responded: "I love hearing that." He then sent a kiss, googly eyes and a heart. He never uses the heart. I sent him the same.

Later another message: "Good morning beautiful. Hope you slept great. Have a fantastic day ahead."

We will see if he responds again today. He said something about running into a problem and it's made my back go up. I'm half expecting a request for some form of help and if that happens, I'm really going to doubt any of what he's said is real.

On one hand I'm hoping my doubts are just based on past experiences—nothing to do with him. That everything he has said to me is real. His feelings and words are real. Boy I really want him and what he's said to be real but in the back of my mind I still have doubts.

Thinking of writing and who texts.

The final thing I hoped wouldn't happen has happened. Sob story and request for money. My response, "sorry I don't have anything—I'm broke trying to get back on solid ground from my ex."

Excerpts from My Journal: September 29, 2019

Last night I shut off my phone because I didn't want the constant barrage. He left several messages asking why I wasn't responding and that he missed me. I responded with: "I turned off my phone because I was very angry that you didn't believe what I told you." His response: "Oh really? Mmmm I see." I then said: "I opened up to you about something." Then he said he believed me. That he thought I cared about him and wanted me to find a way anyways. That he'd give it back ASAP. Plus, I have his cheque so I know he can make good on it. I said "if there was any way I could help you I would." Then he said: "You haven't even tried" and showed some angry faces. Then "Try first."

I said "I do know you could pay me back but honestly have no money available to do that" ($6,200 was what he claimed he needed). He then said, "Or do you not want to help?" I said, "It's not that I don't want to help you. I'm just not in a situation where I can. I don't know why you can't understand/accept that." So, then he says, "It's not all about having the money. It's also about looking for it. It's hard. You're in the free world out there Brenda." I said, "I'm racking my brain to think of something." He said, "I'm counting on it Brenda. I need you more now ... more than I will ever need you. Present and future." I said, "I understand that." He said, "I'm glad you understand. You know how I feel about you. About us. I made up my mind." I ignored that and asked about me depositing his cheque for him. He said, "It needs my presence before it is cleared by the bank. I thought about it and it would have been better if the cheque was for a smaller amount." I said, "Okay that's unfortunate, I guess we continue to think."

Then he changed the conversation to a normal chat. He then asked if I was having a good morning. I said no not really, thinking about him and his issue.

Excerpts from My Journal: October 10, 2019

Since September 29th I've been putting off Will with his money request. Each day he's talking less and less but keeps checking to see if I've left a message for him. I keep stringing him along.

I have to clarify that throughout our conversations I made it very clear I did not have the resources to help him and he needed to find other people to help him out. I wanted him to understand that—regardless of whether he was real or a Catfisher—he was not getting any money from me.

Excerpts from My Journal: October 11, 2019

Will last night was chatty for about an hour before things turned to money. He just doesn't get that I have nothing and I'm okay with that. Putting him off with waiting for the estates to settle then he can have the money he needs— money that I earmarked for a trip to Japan. I really wish I could say for sure that once the money isn't coming, he's going to disappear. I keep looking at his photo, his eyes, and now I see a coldness that I've seen before in military men and so I wonder if Richard is right but seems to get that I don't have it. (Richard is someone who contacted me out of the blue on Skype. He kept pursuing me and I kept telling him I wasn't interested.)

This morning's message was an apology about what's happen and how the money created an issue with us and that he knew we could move past it. That he knew he wants me and my photo is the wallpaper on his phone so he can always look at me. That I'm his everything. He went on and on about how I'm the one he wants and how we being together is all that matters. Just confusing because this isn't the first time he's made it clear he sees me as his. Earlier he had said something about moving from Calgary to be close to his woman. I—the smart ass that I can be—asked "so you see me as your woman?" and he said yes. "Then I have to tell you something you aren't going to like. I've been dating other men." He said why? I said I didn't think we were in some sort of exclusive relationship. He said "I understand." Then I said "I haven't had sex with any of them because you are always at the back of my mind." His response was "I can't wait to fuck you!"

But since he's said things to make it sound like he's head over heels in love. Plus, that he's looking forward to us being together. So not sure if he's trying to convince me or himself that he has someone/something to look forward to. I'm just so confused with him.

Excerpts from My Journal: October 29, 2019

Will sent me this message this morning that just confuses me more about if he's real or not. He keeps giving me messages about how into me he is—doesn't say he loves me—but that he can't wait to be with me. He's still asking for more money but seems to get I don't have it.

Excerpts from My Journal: October 30, 2019

Will last night chatted for about an hour and didn't bring up what he had said. Offered another money solution—cheques from people who owe him paid to me. So, we will see what shows up. This morning his sweet morning was how he hated and favourite part of the day was waking up. He can talk to me when he's awake but his dreams at night are always cut short. Still calling me Sweet Brenda, beautiful, always something. So still unsure if he's real or not.

Excerpts from My Journal: November 3, 2019

Will has been flirty and making it totally nothing about money so not sure. I just don't know with him; I'd love for him to be real but now with Sam I'd have a hard time deciding between the two of them. Sam is someone I met online that lives here and we started talking in September and have been dating.

Excerpts from My Journal: November 4, 2019

Today Will sent messages twice this morning. Now his profile photo is gone from the app we use so not sure what to make of that. His "friend" contacted me about sending money for Will (he called him Wilt) and I found some of his questions questionable and wouldn't answer them. We will see what happens next.

Excerpts from My Journal: November 5, 2019

Will was his sweet self and then started up again about money so I didn't text him and he didn't text me.

Excerpts from My Journal: November 11, 2019

On the 11th I said I missed him and asked for his forgiveness with how short I was with him. He started again about money.

Excerpts from My Journal: November 12, 2019

On the 12th he dropped the request from $1,500 to $500 and then basically called me a liar and selfish (2nd time) and I should go take out a loan at Cash Money or Money Mart.

Excerpts from My Journal: November 13, 2019

On the 13th he basically called me a liar again because I didn't respond to his telling me to take out a loan. My response was "I'm sorry you don't believe me so I'm not going to waste time arguing with you."

Excerpts from My Journal: December 3, 2019

On December 3rd I sent a short message: "Will I miss you." No response.

Excerpts from My Journal: December 6, 2019

Will's response: "Really." I said, "Yes, I miss the sweet Will."

Excerpts from My Journal: December 8, 2019

Will sent me a message from a different phone number but the same app we use: "Hey Brenda." I responded 5 hours later, "Hey Will." 4 hours later he started a conversation to catch up. We chatted for a couple of days and then he started up on money again. He basically tried to make it that I was his only hope and he really needed my help. I asked him about friends and family and he said if he had he wouldn't be asking me. That I need to figure something out and that he adores me. I said I'm glad he adores me but he shouldn't count on me solely for help.

Then the conversation went back to a normal one. He started saying "I'm thinking about you" so I asked about what and he said being with me soon and what he wanted to do with me and my help. I asked him what he wanted to do with me and he asked where I was (he knew I was on my way to work) so when I said on the bus, he said he'd tell me later. He never did, so as usual I ask a question, I get put off and nothing.

Excerpts from My Journal: December 12, 2019

Will and I had been chatting superficially up until this point. He finally started sending me my morning smiles again.

Excerpts from My Journal: December 18, 2019

Even though we'd been talking and he'd been asking about money I finally decided I needed to ask some questions. I still wasn't sure if he's real or not (leaning towards not) but thought maybe some questions would help.

He said he couldn't leave and wasn't sure of his status where he was (I had asked if his visitor/work visa was up) because he owed money for taxes. Again, I told him he needed to stop focusing only on me solving his issue. That I wasn't going to put up with him being pissed off at me for telling him the truth and I wasn't being selfish or lying like he had accused me of in the past. I also said I didn't deal well with demands. I also made the comment that if I "found" some money to give him it would start a never-ending cycle of him expecting me to send him money. He said that if I truly cared for him I would do it. I replied that my feelings had nothing to do with it, that I don't let my feelings overrule my common sense. That my common sense is telling me this is all BS. His response was that I didn't care about him and really SAD!

This started a conversation of about me not being fair to him because of everything we'd been through (?). Ups and downs, plans and now that I didn't trust him—all because of money. I responded it's not all about money and that I had always had doubts about him and what plans? Again, he was vague about what we had planned together. He claimed he was suffering and I asked "then why are you staying there?" He claimed he was there because of his contract and that got derailed by the tax force, that he had lost access to his cash (his ATM and credit cards) and that he was struggling—suffering. I asked if he still had his plane ticket to come back and he said he did. I responded then leave and come back then you can deal with your bank issues and go back to clear stuff up. His response was "don't you think I would if I could, they won't let me leave." His words: "I'm being surveyed."

More questions and answers back and forth and I finally asked "have you contacted the Canadian Embassy to see if they can help you?" He said yes, they had given him some money but it wasn't much help. He promised if I sent money then he would prove me wrong about my doubts. "My coming back ASAP." I explained I want to help but I still have those doubts and maybe I wouldn't have them if we had met in person before he had left. He responded but we've seen each other on video calls several times. That he was honest and all his intentions were pure. That he knows I'm being cautious but he wanted to be here with me.

Since then, back to normal conversations. I'm still unsure if he's real or not. I don't know what will finally give me the answer. Meanwhile I'm in love with Sam. But because Will seems to be a Catfisher, I don't feel guilty about continuing to talk to him.

Sam is real and I know who he is and what he's about—Will is a question mark. I have invested so much time chatting with Will that I need to find out if he is or is not a Catfisher. If he is a Catfisher, my continual conversations with him may save someone else from being manipulated by him. I have feelings for Will. Even though I am writing this book and sharing my journal entries, I want the readers to understand what goes on with these online "relationships." My feelings are real. Will got into my head but not enough to keep me from dating other men, and I was lucky enough to meet and fall in love with Sam.

Chapter 5

Third Contact

This third person who contacted me came from an unexpected source—Pinterest. What made it stranger is that there were two people asking to be contacts with me that I did not know. One was just over the top: he seemed to be a totally made-up personality. When I told him I wasn't interested in him, he wouldn't let it go, and I suggested that he find someone in his area to contact.

Excerpts from My Journal

Number 3, Tim, from Texas, is head over heels with me but I'm not with him. He's a nice guy but totally needy and a giggler. He calls at least once a day. Texts two or three times a day. He's truly a nice guy but again I don't think he's who he says he is.

Tim from Texas.

He is totally on point if he's real. I still have my doubts but I do have strong feelings for him. He's a very sweet man and he's made it clear he's head over heels with me. Unfortunately, he's in Texas but we are supposed to meet in October, him coming here. I had told him I was having surgery so he didn't skip a beat. He said he had to be here for me. Take me to the hospital and take care of me until I'm back on my feet. We will wait and see. He knows I hate winters here so suggested I go there. I said it's an idea to consider, but I wouldn't consider anything like that unless we were in something permanent and he said of course.

So now I'm in a situation I didn't expect. I have strong feelings for both but different one's for each.

I keep going back to Tim—he's dependable, he's been honest (as far as I know). He was in a situation where I thought he'd hit me up for money and *he didn't. The only thing he's said about money is that he makes good money in his job. He has a mortgage so he owns a home. He seems very stable, has a grown son and a grandson and he's close by to his mom. Only bad thing is he works offshore so long hours and away for extended periods of time. He sounds like he's a very normal guy, just a little sheltered and wary of people because of his past. I keep thinking like the last one—if it's feeling too good to be true, it probably is.*

Well he turned out to be another Catfisher. Asked for money at the third week—what is it with these guys thinking after 3 weeks they'll get someone to send money?

He whined and cried about how I didn't really love him or care about him. I finally just stopped responding to him and he didn't pursue it further.

Chapter 6

More Men

I started communicating with another man while I was still talking to Will. Richard contacted me through Skype. It was totally random, and he kept trying to engage me for more than a month. He claimed he was looking up a friend and saw my photo and wanted to talk to me. Given what was going on with Will, I thought, "Hmmm, I know that Will is not what I thought he was, and I know this Richard appears to be another scammer. Let's see what he thinks."

Tebes

Tyler

Richard

Richard asked me if I had a photo of Will, so I sent him one. He responded that he'd seen his photo before, that he's Alcidae and that I should stop talking to him. He then tried to fill in the slot. Richard kept saying he's in love with me and has a "son" who has contacted me and is calling me mom. I don't believe any of it but am waiting for a request for something.

Since then, I've had at least three other scammers and one total nut job contact me.

One guy originally called himself Marc, and later he called himself Tebes. He claimed that he lived in Red Deer (1.5 hours from where I live) and was semi-retired. Of course, he claimed to be an orphan and a widower. The things he was saying to me just didn't ring true, especially when he claimed to have gone on a business trip to New York and the times didn't match up. Then I looked up his photo because he looked familiar to me. It was a photo of the finance minister for Russia! Busted!

Another guy named Tyler contacted me through one dating site. Even though I told him that I wasn't looking for anyone who didn't live in my area, he kept insisting it didn't matter as he was willing to relocate. When I tried to convince him that I wasn't interested, he insisted I was so gorgeous and he had to get to know me. I finally thought, "Okay, let's see where this goes."

I found him to be a total nut job! What I mean by this is he was constantly ignoring what I would say. He had told me he loved his daughter and granddaughter so much, and I said, "Why would you consider leaving them to come to Canada (he's American)?" I never got a response to that. He kept insisting that I take my profile down from all the dating sites I was on. Even though I took myself off the one I met him on, he kept insisting I hadn't. My explanation was that even though I took it down, the site was keeping it up because I had a lot of interest. I finally said "enough" and told him I've removed myself—you can either believe me or not—but I'm not going to be constantly harassed. If you are that insecure, a long-distance relationship isn't going to work for you. He never contacted me again so it was his loss not mine.

After that, William contacted me, and it was only a matter of time before the site we met on contacted me and told me his profile had been taken down and to not continue contact with him. I wasn't really surprised as I had already stopped communicating with him. Because of his profile, I had some sense that he wasn't real but was a Catfisher. His original blurb on his profile said that he was semi-retired and a widower who was relocating from Texas to Edmonton. After a few back-and-forths, he claimed that he was working in Turkey and his daughter had suggested he go online to find someone. In his profile, there was no mention of an adult child or that he was working elsewhere. He listed Edmonton as his home.

Then there was Dave, another one who was "too much too soon." He started talking like we were already in a relationship and that I was his and shouldn't be talking to other men. Once I started questioning things that he was saying, he quickly disappeared.

Charles couldn't even spell his own name. He claimed to be a doctor with the United Nations. Again, I started asking questions and he disappeared.

John texted me on one dating site, and he lived in my general area. We decided to meet for coffee. When I got to the coffee shop, I noticed this beat-up car that circled four times before it finally stopped and parked, but the guy never got out. I waited 20 minutes and then sent the guy a text that I wasn't waiting any longer. The next day he sent me a message that he saw me get out of my vehicle and decided I was out of his league. Seriously!

Excerpts from My Journal: October 10, 2019

Then there is Sam. He lives here and is real. He's decided I'm it in less than a month of chatting, and then finally meeting a couple of weeks ago he started saying he loves me. Tonight, again loves me and can't wait until I'm in his life forever (marriage).

I'm at a loss as to what's next. I had dental surgery on Monday and he spent the night so I wouldn't be alone. He's a very sweet man who loves his job and is a workaholic so it's hard to spend physical time with him. Which causes me to cry and I'm not a crier. As we've talked and getting to know each other he's made it clear he wants to kick my ex's ass for what he did to me. He couldn't believe the mess he left behind or that he wasn't paying all the rent and taking care of me when we were together. Very old fashioned even though he's only one month older than me. He has a good trade, he's a carpenter and a site manager. Owns his own home. Isn't a big spender but not cheap. Should be interesting to see where things go.

I finally had to tell him tonight I'm concerned about all the hours he works and money isn't worth wrecking his health. I think that got to him that I really don't care about finances but care about him. I love his voice—he's Dutch and has a slight accent. I just know he would take care of me and that would be a nice change.

I will limit what I say about Sam because I respect him and our relationship. He is proof that there are good guys that you can meet online.

Excerpts from My Journal: October 11, 2019

A strange start to the day, Richard woke me up around 5:30 with a message which started a sexting session. Oh my God another one who can get me turned on. When we finally finished, he turned the conversation to him coming here in November. As far as he's concerned, I'm his fiancé/wife and he's coming to finalize the deal. He made it clear financially he's going to take care of us (the family including his son). So, the first hint of a request for money and I'm done.

Sam on the other hand texted me when he knew I'm normally up. He's making it clear he's in love and wants me to be in his life forever, so very odd two men who want that.

Excerpts from My Journal: October 29, 2019

Fallen head over heels in love with Sam, but of course, there are 2 others on my mind.

Richard is just so over the top with how "in love" he is with me. But I'm losing interest in him especially when he's asked me to buy him Google Play and Apple cards, which I flat out said no to. Then he wants to come and see me and needs to take "leave" to do so. I got this request for money to pay for paperwork for him to get it. "Bullshit" I said and made it clear I'm not paying it and have no money. I told him bullshit and enough in both English and German (his mother tongue). I told him he needs to figure it out and I'm not able to do it financially and he hadn't told me I'd need to pay for him to come. So now he's "thinking."

So now I'm in a mess of emotions. Sam I can see and touch, and I love to do both. I could totally see myself with him, he makes me smile and laugh. We can talk and I don't worry about him taking things wrong. I know I love him but I don't know if he's the one.

Will, if he's real, we had a connection that I felt before this whole money crap. He's also been in husband mode with me for so long that it would be really easy to go there. I haven't let myself fall in love with him but I can see it happening really quick seeing him in person. I just think if he's real I don't know which I'd pick.

Richard isn't even in the same league as Will and Sam (both my Geminis). At times I think he's a total lunatic and I just don't see me being with him before I'd lose interest and get annoyed by him.

Excerpts from My Journal: October 30, 2019

Richard made no contact all day so I'm thinking I called him out as to what he was—a scam.

Excerpts from My Journal: November 3, 2019

Yesterday finally heard from Richard. Totally avoided the money request, just about how in love with me he was and how a long-distance relationship is hard. That he's always going to love me no matter what. This morning he sent a short message but I responded with very few words so no back and forth conversations.

Excerpts from My Journal: November 4, 2019

Richard has started trying to engage me again. Asked me why I hadn't been texting. If I thought because of the money that he was gone. I said yes and he's "no I love you regardless of when we can be together." So, we will see.

Excerpts from My Journal: November 13, 2019

Needless to say, it means I have no interest in anyone else, including Will, since meeting and getting to know and fall in love with Sam. I sent the last text to Will today because he had been hassling me for money again. I finally told him I'm sorry he doesn't believe I have nothing and that I wasn't going to argue with him anymore.

Excerpts from My Journal: December 4, 2019

Out of the blue (last contact was November 19) Richard tried to video call me and I didn't answer so he texted and I responded. Still wanting me to send money so he can be with me for Christmas. I said no I didn't want company for Christmas, that I was stressed out at work and didn't need more stress. He ignored what I said and pushed for money again. I said, "There is no money Richard so it's not going to happen. It's going to have to wait until your contract is done and you have access to your finances." His response was "OMG" and then no more text. After 28 minutes I texted, "So I guess your love was based on money so it wasn't real."

Since this last journal entry, the following has happened:

Will and I still have some limited contact, but now I'm sure he is a Catfisher. The reason why I finally came to this conclusion is that it's very clear that I'm not speaking only to the person I originally was. I think there are now three Wills. One for sure has very limited knowledge of English and how to use it. The other one doesn't seem to understand what I'm saying either. The original Will occasionally comes on line but it's happening less and less. I also found a photo that Will had sent me using the name Jeff and Todd online.

Richard has finally understood that there is no money coming from me to him. I get the occasional text by phone or on the app we had been talking on. He still says he loves me.

Sam and I are together and planning a future together. He knows about this book and supports me in writing in it. He trusts that I'm not going to indefinitely continue to text with these other guys. Once our plans are more solid and this book his finished, Will and Richard will get a text from me saying goodbye.

Chapter 7

Warning Signs

There are many common warning signs that you need to be aware of when you look for love online. Here is my list:

1. Men who are not physically where you are. If you can't arrange to meet them, you are putting yourself at risk. After the first six men that were questionable, I made a rule that I don't give out my phone number or email address until I meet someone face to face. People lie on their profiles about their locations so insisting on meeting face to face can help you weed out the liars.

2. Men who claim to be widowers. I found it so hard to believe that there were that many men on websites looking for women who had lost their wives (and in many cases their only child). Statistically, women outlive men, so it makes you wonder.

3. Men who claim to be retired. Given the economy, anyone under 60 who claims to be retired may more likely be unemployed.

4. Men who are too quick to give a sob story about themselves. Sob stories are often about how they have been given a raw deal, such as a cheating wife/girlfriend, an untimely job loss or a death. Most

men don't give personal details until they know the person they are talking to.

5. Men who claim to be in love with you too soon. This is a tough one because we all want to hear someone is in love with us. If it happens too soon, it's probably not real, especially if you have never met each other in person or video calls.

6. Men who want to be with you too quickly. I had one man who not only thought we were meant to be together but talked like we had been together and I should want him to come "home."

7. Men who have "business trips" early in the "relationship." It's usually the first sign that eventually they are going to create some sort of issue or situation that they need you to help with or solve.

8. Men who have "unexpected emergencies." I've been told that while on a "business trip" they can't access their bank credit cards and or ATM cards so they need my financial help.

9. Men who are overbearing. They may have the belief that as the man you should do as they say and be happy that they are paying any type of attention to you and are considering having a relationship with you.

10. Men with photos that don't match up. The first Catfisher I was involved with had a profile photograph that was not the same person that I eventually got photographs of. The photo I eventually wound up getting were the same consistent person (I could tell by the smile) but the ages of the man were very different. In the first photo, he looked around the age he said he was, but towards the end it was clearly a much younger man and the photos were Photoshopped.

11. Photos can also be Photoshopped to show the person you are communicating with in various places or situations. You can use Google Images to check and see if the photo is of the place, they

claim it is. One of the men I was in contact with Photoshopped himself in various places but he repeatedly used the same photo and pose of himself (if it was actually him). Another posted a photo that was in front of a blank screen, totally setting himself up to plug himself into another photo (idiot!).

12. Inconsistent use of language. It became very apparent to me with some of these men that I was speaking to more than one person. The use of certain words seemed to be inconsistent as well as how they would word things. Even pet names were not consistent.

13. Statements that rub you the wrong way. What many of these Catfishers don't understand is that saying certain things in their culture may be fine, such as the way males speak to women. But for a North American woman, it may sound condescending and chauvinistic.

Chapter 8

What to Do If You Suspect You Are Being Groomed

Catfishers groom their victims before they ask for money. Being groomed means that you are developing a relationship where there is trust and an emotional connection. The bottom line is that Catfishers are in the business of going after money—not love.

The process could be something as simple as asking you to do a small thing (like in my case accepting a piece of mail for them. It may be a number of small things that don't seem to be anything major but it's a form of testing to see if you are under their "spell". That you will blindly do what they ask without thinking or questioning it.

Or they could ask questions that aren't appropriate for a casual contact to ask. Catfishers often don't answer your questions. This drove me crazy. If it's okay for you to ask questions about me, you should reciprocate, and if you don't, why not?

I began to suspect that my first contact was a Catfisher when his communications changed. I suspected that I was being talked to by more than one person and that there were actually three people answering me. I could actually begin to tell which one I was talking to by their language, what they asked me and how they addressed me. There was one who had good English skills, one that was a sex fiend and the third one clearly struggled with English.

Another tactic for grooming is to keep you sleep-deprived. Catfishers do this by saying they are in another time zone and then calling you, texting you and Skyping you at times when you should be sleeping. I repeatedly told one of the guys I was involved with about the time difference and said I was going to shut off my phone while I was sleeping because he was waking me up. He responded, "I love you so much I forget to look at the time and when it is where you are." I said, "That's sweet but I'm not a nice person when I don't get enough sleep, so please stop." Of course, he didn't stop, and I kept my ringer off so I wouldn't get woken up.

Talk to your family and trusted friends about the person you are in contact with. They can be much more objective about what is going on than you can. They will be able to see warning signs that you may be missing or ignoring, such as a complete stranger who is messing with your feelings, hopes and wants.

Question what is being said to you, especially if you are being asked to send money to "help" with a situation. Do not believe you are the only one that can help them; do not believe the situation they claim to be in; and most importantly do not send money.

Chapter 9

Stop and Think about What Is Being Said to You

On the most basic level, you need to carefully listen and read what is being said to you to see if it sounds like it's real, possible and believable. Sometimes when you simply walk away for a minute to think about it, you're going to see the cracks. I found that the minute I was told certain things, my back would go up and I was suspicious of what was being said. Even if the Catfishers hadn't asked for money then and there, I suspected that it was going to happen. And when it did, I wasn't as surprised and I was ready to say no.

All of the guys that were Catfishers were really bad at keeping track of what they said. This was even clearer when there was more than one of them talking to me. An example is repeating questions but with different words. For that reason alone, I never deleted my conversations with them so I could go back and analyze what was being said. With the first Catfisher, it was clear there was more than one person I was talking to. Even with Will, there were times when the language wasn't consistent. For example, normally he would use the word "you" but other times there would be "U" instead.

Bad English is a warning sign. Many of the Catfishers' language skills are poor but not bad enough to see right away. But you will notice their word usage is often not appropriate. I found myself asking for clarification on something that was said. On the other hand, they would ask me to clarify something that I said because they didn't understand the reference I used or what I was talking about. North Americans have different dialects and word usage that can't be taught to someone learning English as a second language. If you carefully look at the texts you are sent, you may be able to detect that someone is claiming to be American or Canadian, but you will see their word usage will stand out.

Another warning sign was talking to you in a way that rubs you the wrong way. For me, I hate being called dear. You are not my elderly aunt, so it's not appropriate to talk to me and call me dear. I've always found it a condescending word and don't like being called it by anyone. I said this to one Catfisher, and he disappeared.

Talk to your family and friends and ask what they think. Don't be embarrassed about asking for someone else's opinion. They aren't emotionally involved so can be a lot more objective.

Chapter 10

Call the Catfisher Out

In order to give yourself closure, you need to make a statement to the Catfisher so he knows you know what he is. He needs to know that you are done with them. Be specific: tell him exactly what he did and how it made you feel. He may not have the capacity to understand or have remorse but at least you will get it off your chest.

I haven't done this with all of them, but I was passive aggressive with the ones I didn't call out by not responding to them anymore. This was not truly satisfying because in order to get closure I needed to call them out. My advice is to call them out as Catfishers.

An example of this is I called Richard out by saying I did not believe that his employer would require him to have a lawyer draw up documents for him to take leave from his job. Further I told him I have never paid for something my employer required me to do (even doctor notes I pay up front and I am reimbursed for them). If his employer was engaging a lawyer to draw up legal documents, they should be paying them not "us". I found it ridiculous that the "lawyer" was basing his fee on where he was taking his leave at. It just made absolutely not sense to me and I refused to be a part of such nonsense! He claimed he had contacted his employer and another employee and that was the norm, I said well he'd have to figure out things himself I wasn't going to be involved.

Chapter 10

Call the Catfisher Out

In order to give yourself closure, you need to make a statement to the Catfisher so he knows you know what he is. He needs to know that you are done with them. Be specific: tell him exactly what he did and how it made you feel. He may not have the capacity to understand or have remorse but at least you will get it off your chest.

I haven't done this with all of them, but I was passive aggressive with the ones I didn't call out by not responding to them anymore. This was not truly satisfying because in order to get closure I needed to call them out. My advice is to call them out as Catfishers.

An example of this is I called Richard out by saying I did not believe that his employer would require him to have a lawyer draw up documents for him to take leave from his job. Further I told him I have never paid for something my employer required me to do (even doctor notes I pay up front and I am reimbursed for them). If his employer was engaging a lawyer to draw up legal documents, they should be paying them not "us". I found it ridiculous that the "lawyer" was basing his fee on where he was taking his leave at. It just made absolutely not sense to me and I refused to be a part of such nonsense! He claimed he had contacted his employer and another employee and that was the norm, I said well he'd have to figure out things himself I wasn't going to be involved.

Chapter 11

How to Extract Yourself from Catfishing

Once you realize you are being preyed upon and want to get away, it's much harder than you or most people would think. You have developed feelings for this person and a routine around your contact with them. You have made plans with the Catfisher. You may feel angry or sad and that's normal. You will probably go back and forth numerous times with questions as to whether they real or not and whether you should cut ties with them and that's normal.

The best way to extract yourself once you know that the person is a Catfisher is to block them. Block their phone number, email, Skype accounts and all others. They may try to contact you through other accounts, especially if you made the mistake of sending them money. The best defense is to not respond.

If you know for sure that you were being Catfished, contact the online dating site you met them on and give them the heads up. Odds are you aren't the only one they've contacted, and the site isn't going to want to continue to give them the platform to continue.

Remind yourself that you opened yourself to the possibility of love and it's not your fault that there are people in the world who are always out to profit from others. You go in with pure thoughts and intentions, but the people you may come in contact with didn't contact you with the same intentions. You go into it with the thoughts of love and don't expect to be taken advantage of.

Chapter 12

Forgive Yourself

We often blame ourselves when things go wrong. But you were brave enough to venture online and put yourself out there, which is powerful. Remember that strength if you find yourself being dragged into a Catfisher's trap. You need to understand that they are professionals at what they do, and they have a lot of experience with saying all the right things to mess with your mind. Unfortunately, some people make the mistake of giving them money before they realize that they are being scammed. Consider it the price to pay to learn.

Here is an example of how these Catfishers will escalate a situation and mess with you:

Tim, the guy I met on Pinterest, originally started out as just wanting to be friends because he liked and was interested in my Pinterest boards. We had a casual conversation on Pinterest, and then he asked if we could talk on Hangouts because there we could talk back and forth easier. I agreed to it and we had basic back-and-forth conversations.

On Day 4, I had the first warning sign that maybe I wasn't the only one he was talking to when he called me "Elizabeth." I said, "Elizabeth?" He right away said, "Oh sorry, I made a mistake." Yes, it was a mistake that clued me in that I wasn't the only one he was talking to, despite him telling me that he didn't have any friends because he had had a bad experience with one that had been jealous of him. This put my back up.

On Day 20, all of a sudden there was a mention of a "problem" at work. A piece of equipment he used in his work broke down and couldn't be fixed. The replacement cost was $114,000. He claimed it was his equipment and therefore he had to pay to replace it.

Surprise, surprise! On Day 23 he claimed to be in love with me.

On Day 24, he started talking more about how he needed money for a replacement part and what he was doing to try and get the money.

On Day 25, he said a friend was helping with some money (after he'd already told me he had no friends).

Day 28 was the first time he actually asked me for money. I made it clear I didn't have any nor would be able to give him anything and why. He wouldn't stop asking me, and I was at work. Finally, I told him he was harassing me and I wasn't going to respond any more to him.

Not surprisingly, I never heard from him again, so my only conclusion was it was all about money!

This is why I say you need to forgive yourself. These Catfishers are good at getting into your head. If you aren't paying attention to what they are saying, you can be fooled.

Chapter 13

How to Protect Yourself

First and foremost, when you enter the online dating world, be aware that not everyone is honest and not everyone is looking to find someone with love or friendship on their mind. You must decide how much of your personal information you are willing to share in your profile. Looking back now, I realize I gave too much information—it was basically bait for the Catfishers. I gave information that made me look like an easy target for them, such as the fact that I had never been married, had no children, and was educated and employed. Now, I would put only basic information in my profile, such as my age and some things I was interested in. I would also clearly state I did not want to be contacted by anyone outside of the country or not within a certain distance from where I lived.

Second, do not give out your email or phone number to anyone until you meet them in person. After you physically meet them, you can get a good idea if you want to continue contact with them. You need to trust your instincts, and your instincts work better when you can be face to face with someone. During a Skype call, they can claim to be anywhere, and they can actually be anywhere in the world. Moreover, you can't get a true read on someone until you are in the same physical space.

Third, do not believe everything these people say to you. Critically think through what they say to you and ask a lot of questions. I was brought up such that you shouldn't ask a lot of personal questions especially of people you don't know. In online dating, you need to protect yourself by asking a lot of questions. Don't be afraid to do it, and if someone is offended by it, so be it. If they ignore or don't answer your questions, odds are because they are hiding something.

Fourth, beware of certain phrases that are said too soon. Examples are: "You are always on my mind" and "I've never felt like this before with a woman." "I can't believe how quickly I've fallen in love with you." I heard these phrases from all of the Catfishers.

Fifth, as time goes on, the Catfishers will amp up their game and make it sound like you are their one and only and as a result you should be more than willing to do anything for them. They will remind you that you have made plans for a future together and then try to blame you that you played with their minds. They may claim that you had plans to have a future with them. They may say that if you were really serious about them and the "relationship," then you would do anything and everything to make them happy.

It's all a big game. The end goal of these Catfishers is always to get something from you. Once they get something, they will keep coming after you for more. Remember that.

Chapter 14

Closure

I was so angry, disgusted and unhappy that someone actually targeted me (not once but numerous times) and thought they could manipulate me. What made me so mad was that these Catfishers have no concept of what sort of manipulation they are doing to another human being. This experience could scar the person they target for the rest of that person's life. Financially, they could also ruin this person's life if they go to extremes to give the Catfishers the money they request.

I believe that these types of people are cowards and they do this manipulation online because it's impersonal and they don't have to see the person face to face and the devastation that their behaviour causes. Most of the Catfishers I was in contact with seemed to be under the impression that all of us North Americans are rich. Thus, what they are asking for shouldn't be an issue and we should gladly give them whatever they wanted. As I was employed by the government, they thought I had it made and had endless money. Thus, there shouldn't be any issue with me dropping whatever amount of money they asked for.

My experiences spurred me to write this book to save others from similar experiences.

Disclaimer

Please note that the images of men in this book were photos "they" sent me. I do not believe they were used with permission of the real persons the photos portray. If the people in my book were real and I identified them as Catfishers, I am sorry. However, your behaviour caused me to believe you were just that.

If you would like to contact me about these images, please email me at brendaleeacheson@outlook.com.

www.ingramcontent.com/pod-product-compliance
Lightning Source LLC
LaVergne TN
LVHW042000060526
838200LV00041B/1809